Soul's Flight

SOUL'S FLIGHT

NANCY MACKENZIE

Ekstasis Editions

Canadian Cataloguing in Publications Data

Mackenzie, Nancy
Soul's flight

Poems.
ISBN 1-896860-04-4

I. Title.
PS8575.K4227S68 1997 C811'.54 C97-910834-6
PR9199.3.M3285S68 1997

Acknowledgements:
Some of these poems have been published in the following journals and magazines: *Hecate's Loom, The Capilano Review, Blue Buffalo, Dandelion, Prairie Fire,* and *Fields of Gold.*

Soul's Flight was written with the assistance of a grant from the Alberta Foundation for the Arts

Published in 1997 by:
Ekstasis Editions Canada Ltd
Box 8474, Main Postal Outlet
Victoria, B.C., V8W 3S1

Ekstasis Editions
Box 571
Banff, Alberta T0L 0C0

Soul's Flight has been published with the assistance of a grant from the Canada Council and the Cultural Services Branch of British Columbia.

Contents

Dedication

For my mother and my father.

For mom who asked why do you write? and

For dad who is the true visionary of the family.

The soul is a traveller
that sleeps every night in another inn.

Plotinus, Third Century AD

To the extent that the soul turns towards itself and towards divine things and shows that it has its own motions, which may surmount the corporeal condition, it testifies too that it does not depend on the body and that it agrees with divine things and that therefore, separated from the body, it can live united with divinity.

The human animal can be called both immortal and mortal: immortal insofar as it consists of a rational soul and its celestial body, mortal insofar as it is joined to an elemental body. But any mundane god is an absolutely immortal animal. Socrates therefore warns us lest we perhaps be deceived when we consider the composition of an immortal animal. We suppose that a mundane god is an animal with a soul and body naturally and perpetually joined. This is true up to a point, but we do not comprehend it with any certain reason, particularly if we ever conceived of this union in terms of the intercourse between the soul and mortal, earthy body. For the latter is not utterly ready for life. Instead of the body approaching the soul, the soul is borne down to the body in a headlong fall and sustains it only with effort and governs it with care. Yet this does not happen with the soul and the celestial body. For the latter turns towards the soul with a sort of wonderful readiness in the same way as the soul turns towards it, as Plotinus frequently maintains. The elemental body does not possess the power to receive life to the degree that the soul has to bestow life; so it does not live forever, nor is it entirely nor perfectly whole. The celestial body, however, does possess the power to the same degree; so it seizes the whole life equally and wholly and preserves it forever.

The soul is the fountain and principle of movements: fountain, since as universal motion it perpetually flows out of itself, into itself, and into others; principle, since it effectively controls what is in motion.

Texts II, *Commentarium in Phedrum*, the Prague Manuscript,
by Marsilio Ficino (Florence, 1496)

Angel

I have no further questions, just a plea: not yet
not illumination

imagine this intricate situation,
saturate with power
solid, scary
inspired

an image, a being realer than real
not in the mirror
quiet
present
come for

an ancient comfort, mother to mother
I remember you holding me thus
caressing me thus
comforting me thus

holding me

and when the glorious skies open with light and smote
a sacrifice
if ever there was one
a talisman
ethereal and transient

an angel

Day One, Venice

Dad, did you think we could, together, bring Mom back?
wherever two or three are gathered together in my name

Christ is a name we don't often hear in conversation
yet yesterday I overheard it

as two old men walked round and round our neighborhood
heads bowed then lifted to the heavens

will the sky beholden of ancient gods lift our hearts
Mediterranean sun, Dad, and no, she won't be there

standing in awe in Florence
head thrown back to the magnificent David

we'll have enough praying to do every night before dinner
each day at a different port, the ship taking us from pew to pew

and I will stand before your altar
with the travel plan in hand

altered for the living, with destinations to plan
when we are at home together far far from this land

All that dies
has first to live

Bruce Cockburn, Twentieth Century

Memorial Service

the minister is a Scottish fellow
who says the Lord is my shepherd in lowland Scots
the laird is my herd,
Jack Brown sings "The Road to the Isles", a Scottish song
as well as "Morning Has Broken", a Gaelic song

there is no casket and the service is short
but it marks something for the public
they can see the family gathered in black
we talk to friends and neighbours
dispense with all the flower arrangements
bring home trays of uneaten sandwiches

it isn't really an end at all, it isn't really a beginning, either
what is memorable, unfortunately, are
the three weeks before the service and the months afterwards

months afterwards with a black raven
sitting on the barbed wire fence

and a bird of prey, too

Oh Lucky Owl

where I walk
in slow and even steps
my imprints on sage, thistle,
gallardi and fescue
gone in a moment
the toes of my boots soaked through
with mid-morning dew
I thought I heard an owl in the willows
and follow the wending cattle path
toward the crackling boughs
of old willows and wing flaps.

What, I wonder, would Cora
make of all these owls?
Each night one roosts on the porch,
annoying with its crazy hoot
Why did we ever think the owl wise?
and luck?
It was our luck to remember Pollyanna
strapped to a chair
the walking doll scares away
that bird of prey
no more clicking of the jowls as it feeds and decapitates
on the porch

Before the Fall

Before the three weeks there was everything

there was family growth, new motherhood
getting used to mom calling me mom

there were gardens and annuals, seeds to be sown
trips to the kennels, the dog growing too old

there was a firing, and a lawsuit
a big Hanoverian gelding and two dressage instructors
my diet and the baby being born

the moon and the stars, mother playing cards
a fortnight in Hawaii,
mahi mahi on the barbeque, the
let's do this again next year

there was the Thanksgiving when I drank too much
with a headache the next day
walking out for solace to the big wheat field

the wind biting cold
the sky huge as a manuscript

finding a round bale to shelter in
slumping in the straw

two puppies roaring round
mother joining me to talk

wearing sunglasses against the bright sky
God shining down on us

a flock of trumpeter swans arcing over

talking about *everything*
God and love and families

there was my father out with the weed eater
cleaning up the roadway
out fixing the barbed wire fences, watering the cattle

there was my husband
out every morning walking the dogs in a romp
around the perimeter of the fields,
cutting across to the big dug-out so the dogs could swim
Mom giving the dogs a bath at night,
black hairs all over the marble tile in the bathroom

there were Leslie and Brad coming out to the big house
to stay up late playing billiards
listening and dancing to old jazz

there were Jim and Liz
with their two kids,
everyone and everything
before the three weeks that she lay dying.

Angel Poems

An Angel in the Garden

Calendula, Artemisia
Absinthium
powers of flowers
herbs and healing
back me on this: I'm betting
on the curative powers of nature
not nurture

mother's gone, it's natural
with the passing of time
for a mother's back to ache
bear down on the muscles
my husband gives a good back rub
the passage of souls in flight

wind chimes sound in their passing

We brought the baby home
on a blustery, icy day and at night, with the storm clouds
the vortex of wind in the yard fighting into the house,
mother went out into the yard
took the wind chimes down
laid them in the garden

perhaps a huge angel
enveloped within its wings
slipped behind her as she came in from the cold

all night the angel stood in our hallway

why did it stay for four days?
it's too late to tell
it left when mom left   me propped with pillows
on the queen-sized bed
nursing the baby   and Mom came back into the room

a catch in her throat
to hug and kiss us one more time, then out, out with the angel
to the snow and cold, the drive to Loch End, we were left

eerily alone in the calm nursing silence
transmigration of souls
take this, and eat

part of my soul flew with you, Angel
south and west

today, I am speechless,
my grief an echo
of wind chimes chiming in the garden

Death of an Angel

Do angels die? Like Lucifer, an angel could fall
shooting star, faltering light turning from God to darkness

What of animals? We always thought that one of our horses
having lived and died among us, would come
carry the light burden of our freed souls to the light of heaven
even Beautiful Joe would be there

She lay there dying and I
watching out the picture window
saw the snow-clad landscape
listened to the sound of her laboured breathing
waited for the moment of her death
a process not unlike the birthing of my child

when she was awake, I asked if she remembered
the horses galloping over the hills
I expected Miss Lucky
or Simalite, one of the earlier thoroughbred broodmares
Mom had made a pact with one of them long ago
which one it was I never knew

a story told in cross-stitch
a tapestry woven by her gnarled and lovely hands
the story over the bedstead showed a rider
a beautiful girl on a white horse

she slept. I walked from the room and roamed.
Dad asked me in the bleak night
where was my big angel now
I felt luckless and useless
wandering around the ranch house
calling out to the angels
clucking to the horses in the field
and finally found on the hallway's wooden floors
that fallen feather
the shaft long and white and perfect
feather weighted with silken gold
the tip of the feather broken and clipped

from an unharnessed horse
that wouldn't come home?

I to the Hills

Mother, were you my flight stabilizer, my arrow?

what flight were you sent on in the early foggy night?
I flew, not from you
so much as to sanctuary, to rest

my family, in the dark, foggy night, asleep or sleeping
falling into
out of the night
air, fog and the hills
the hills whisking us away up and down
ponds thawing
mists settling unsettling in fact
the tip of an arrow
does it really matter? Mother?
the tree trunk you hug
the mother of the forest
the arrow from the forest

would there by substance be an arrow
rooted in my heart?
yes, and more

there is more
there is everything that matters, there is more, there is mother
there are the hills, the fog, the driving up and down the hills
to get to the house
who is she anyway asks my brother
he is behind the wheel
and we are driving very fast

and I am forever driving to and from her death
an arrow in my heart

Soul's Flight

I

There is a photo of Andrew and Babe
I took in Taormina, Sicily
in a ruin (monastery) overlooking Mount Etna
taken in 1992, near the first of October
when, if family folklore is true
my mom was still on her flight to heaven

and we stood on the deck of the *Song of Norway*
raised a champagne glass on her birthday
and cheered her on many of us
immensely sad; I think it rained

II

here's something to remember your mother by
a small rose bush

how did my neighbour know
in dying mom ran for the roses like a Kentucky Derby horse
although her race was from pain
her run unto death

III

Eulogy 2: March 7, 1996

Good day, Mom. God speed, Mom. God love you, Mom. Love you, Mom. Miss you.

We're still running for the roses.

IV

I remember how the angel said *not yet*
and I thought it had come for the baby
not yet, I begged
and in acquiescence to me
the angel waited with us
a small girl spirit in the bedchamber
similarly over the makeshift crib by the stairs
all separate times, these visitations,
while Mom's spirit flew

V

"when the light that's lost within us
reaches the sky"
— Jackson Brown,1974, *Late for the Sky*

VI

limitless
the possibilities
boundless
the perimeter
undefined
existence
rapture

capture a raptor
tether to your gloved hand
jest about it with the others
even your mother
wouldn't understand

I've sewn you here into this tapestry
you move with the grace of a dressage rider
all across the field with medieval charm
questing, hunting, jousting, riding with a jingle and a jangle
of bits and spurs, creak of leather
flap of wing and snap of banner
in the binding wind
you move with a purpose
even your mother wouldn't understand

VII

God, the archer, let loose the arrow
say it went through life
kept going, clean on to its target
through the night, through the hills
to the sky, to the One Beyond

Ritual

In this city of hierarchies, the angels have been forgotten

slow and military, there is advance
or quick back-step innuendo

I fall
into pattern
in a little hermitage in the woods
where the shape feet trace on the floor
opens abbey or abyss
and the ritual is the same:
distorted by the treacherous floor

floor or earth, ribbons of water and mud
green growing reeds/brilliant snow,
high trees or willow silhouette
the raven calls
and I circle round a flame.

quiet pattern in the woods over, on a bamboo plate painted
in calligraphic words
I crush two-year-old sage
and the black messenger of war
glides through the snowfall
to a mansion over the border

Wise Woman

My wise woman
is a reference book
and my primitive culture
the CBC

icons for pagans
wisdom gone in the twinkling of an eye
constellatory myths beseeching me

speak out against the poverty of progress
usurpation of commercial class
spiritless voids of concrete and glass
mirrored back reality
my face shining at the window

Going down to mend the fences
where the Morgan gelding runs
round the corrals, weathered wood
blue or gray for mountains or sky
fences or sloughs
circular catches of water for blue heron
muskrats, the bulrush too
prairie the seasons, steers
brown, aye almost blue ones
bellies scraping the grass
the salt around the tongue

speak out against the poverty of progress
usurpation of commercial class
spiritless voids of concrete and glass
mirrored back reality
the stars overhead
wheeling with a music of their own

Recognition

homing back into town
the city stretches before me
Terwillegar Drive, like a salamander
snakes beneath the car lights
elemental river and sky
meet at my back door
the bridge, en route, is unoccupied

only the country smell remains
of the stables, my boots
at the landing
track manure and straw
into the house

here, inside the pulsing lights of the city,
I imagine there are other rooms
where others sit before their windows
looking out at the lights
a reflection of the solitude they feel
squared up inside those book-lined rooms

I sit before a fire, wrapped in my bathrobe,
a blanket around my knees
Enalyion at the hearth
a brandy in hand

even as the crystal catches a glimpse
of a gaze, it is gone, gone back into reflective thought

my book, from 1496, Florence:

> *Instead of the body approaching the soul,*
> *the soul is borne down to the body in a headlong fall*
> *and sustains it*
> *only with effort and governs it with care*

the city is a distant crystal
I am inside the light

so, in their indomitable ways, Plotinus, Ficino
show me the roots of my humanity
the trajectory of a soul in flight
essences and basics
the highest form of light shining through darkness

I twirl the stem of the crystal between forefinger and thumb
hum

stare back at my reflection in the light
the night, with its icy earthly   smells
keeps circling with the stars

out there on the winding trail back to the stables
some cars still travel on the packing snow
over the bridge
their lights catching, briefly, the swirls of lace

and the sheer potentiality of others
sitting thus
knee clad before their somber windows
fire crackling on the hearths
roadways intersecting between here and there
sheer, cold, potential reality

ah but such thoughts are obscure
and I shelve them
close my eyes
remember there is a tomorrow
then we'll all see more clearly
when the white day dawns
the city stretching itself in a blanketed
morning and
a sun that will rise with a fire of its own

Mother,
You have made me

New Poetry

Yes, I've thought about the artistry of raising children
and cringe a little at the responsibility
it's not easy being a living work of art

first mom said "perhaps I spent too much time
keeping my house in order
when I could have spent more time with you kids"

then she said that her contribution to the world
was three wonderful children who could
contribute to the world

however, I know that this is not the whole story
because if mom had spent less time doing housework
and more time painting, sketching, sculpting
sewing, and dreaming up new projects
she would have left even more of a legacy
a lasting monument to her own talents

works of art stand alone with a signature
affixed somewhere to assert the artist's ownership

where on my body is there room for a signature?
and where on my child's body is there room for this tattoo?

The Critic

The critic said that there had to be more of a story
sing it out! shout it out! but tell it somehow!

so let me spell it out, to myself, if I can
it goes something like this:

Jesus loves me this I know
for the Bible tells me so

little ones, like my baby, like the child inside of me
aka my soul know something of Christ
and question uncomprehendingly why souls
are entire of themselves, yet yearn endlessly for unity

soulmate mother you bore me and raised me
by your hand another mother born

till now you have had many of the answers
more of the questions of life and religion

hug that huge poplar in the field
the mother tree, teach me anew your simple beliefs
that I may pass on those simplicities to my children
that I may still always be your baby
even in your absence, even with your soul aflight

somehow tell me a story for I am weary
your hand on my brow
twiddling my shorn bangs
in the nightlight the quilt around me
tell me a bed-time story

Kitchen Easel

Set them up beside me today, please
I'll just sit child-like at the kitchen table
you might want an easel, several paintbrushes, and oils

dance lightly at your easel, mix strong colours on your pallet

white, tawny wheat brown, green black for evergreens, gray blue for shadows and depth, royal blue for peeking sky, and something for the distance

your canvas, I think
should be large
something landscape shaped
to encompass this foothills view

I'll sit by you and train the telescope
on anything that moves
that herd of deer in the barley field
a gyrfalcon on a round bale of straw
catch the slant of two fallen trees

with a quick stroke of your brush
paint Phil and the Dobermans
and Enalyion struggling through drifts
an old dog who's lost her country sense
flailing as she fails to skirt the drifts
paint that in if you can

where the willow stands are tinged orange
and an old dead pine marks one of the best view spots on the land
look toward it, draw it in, a focal point to looking past
to the dark green along the Bill Hill Springs Road

paint in the slopes of the entry ravine
where the sun shines on the tree girt slopes
and the plateau is dark and flat and even
flow that horizon line north and west
up over the golden straw bales flecking the fields
find Hamish's hill and colour in
the Grand Valley with its long-standing farm houses

Today you won't be able to paint the mountains
so leave them out
they aren't there to paint
just use white for the incoming sky
why? because this is the new Strome Glen Farm
and though we know the mountains are there
wrapped in the wispy snow clouds in the west

we're struggling each year to inure this new farm
with a past that lays down like shooters and roots
we're bothered by Mother's illness
baby's crying, family separations
and potentialities of divorce

why paint this simple landscape
in its mutable weather-wise form?
it has its constancies of moment
its shadows following the trailing sun

Generations

I go down south where the spirit winds blow
to revive my parched and forgotten soul
I go down to drive over gravel roads
to pause by an owl's nest and count the young
to yearn when all yearning is done
I go down to sit in the forests

terraced hills and diamond willow
Dad and I watch for the great horned owl
the high bare limbs of the willow and poplar
leaves crackling underfoot
dogs run on by
wind an absent force in the fall forest
we guess it must be roosting away from its nest
and walk back up the hill to home

mother you have made me
naive again
and again an innocent

bring on the awful angels
sing out praise to the earth
this is a poem I wrote
before you went to the earth

life is never over
if you believe as my grandmother does
in predestination and in life everlasting
why else is she still alive
senile
a spirit trapped in a body that cries?

I notice that Granny's face is dark with blood
she has just come from her bath
gives that little sniff of indignation
as slowly we all cluster round her
silent in the face of her supposed dying
talk is to one another
inarticulate and lapsing

in each caressing moment
of this life we may be closer
touching souls
going down into each other
running in the four circles of life
down south

we were brought together again
who were not yet torn apart
and I believed that Granny would die first
she survived you, and still
you make me young, a child, your baby
each time I think of you
and whenever I see or hear
the great horned owl
roosting

Needlepoint

Mother has captured the Blue Boy
in an infamous pose
flat on his back in the meadow
with his white shirt rumpled and free

Mother, will you add
two faces - yours and mine
and all those other present
on the flower field

the dusk rushing in on her answer,
she is ruddy cheeked and smiling
at the children and dogs causing havoc

consider and pause
when she stopped time stopped

for the sewer had to fill in all of the faces
long tapered fingers poised with needle and thread

shadows of shaded yellow
orange and brown
a blue for the gathering night
pale blue pond in the distance
and a dark dark moon
Mother captured the afternoon

The Yarn

Bury the thread deep
in the pocket of my throat
find out how to save things
by saying nothing.

Keep the hiding place
of caragana

hedges a secret.

Thimbleless and coatless
bereft of all
qualms about secrecy
skate,
trace
a name in ice.

Yes, there is much that cannot be seen
the thorns on roses in winter
the flash of needle between lips.

Where blood seeps through the stitches
where others have walked the paths
the lifeline tangles.

Find my ancestry through stories
the petit point pictures mother did
in pregnancy

rocking, rocking
settled
midway in velvet and dream
thinking, doubtless
this is only one side of things
as if the back of the picture
is loose threaded knots.

Dusk

there is a stupid owl in the willows
where abysmal calls cleft the earth
where fountains a lucifer
the other side of night approaching

over and over the same cry retreats
to golden social calls the demands
of white the evil of purity

sagacious and awful owl
sophia of the foothill's dusk

the horse in the rain stands mute
though the owl
and the rain of stars
light the barnyard
the pigeon's coo coo
stupid in the essential rise of a full moon in May

we can all be stars in the crazy moonlight
falling and grating upon each other

like wood that creaks before the sparks and smoke
a bough creaking as the great bird takes flight
wings dark and flapping in the darkening forest

Late Night

late in the night, when everyone else is asleep, mother and I sit up and talk. we discuss philosophical things like what does it all mean? what is my life, what is our life? and we manage to find positive meaning to life, we allow for the sanctity of animal life and the joy of pets. There is this house and the silence as it breathes, there is the presence of this family, security, Dad sleeping with a loaded shotgun by his bed, a German Shepherd at the door

late night. stars wheel. grandfather clock tolls
late night talking

I remember going downstairs for ice or
to let the dogs in or to check
on some distant noise from the barn

mom waiting upstairs, patient, omnipresent,
comfortingly there

and taking my time about it, Dad asleep in his bed
the house expansive and breezy
the floodlight switches arrayed in the hallway
and the household gods at the door

looking out, hands on either side of the doorframe
breathing and smelling and wakening
with the munching of cattle, the rustle of horses in paddocks
the barn, framed in the barnlight and moonlight
my mare laying down on the straw

and tearing myself away from the world outside
a dog's wet paw treading across my bare feet
clutching my flannel pyjamas and walking down the long hall
to the stairs
completely forgetting all else but the next moment of philosophy

my mother and I of an evening
would sit upstairs and talk

Rune Stones, Message of Death

I should have seen it coming, she told us long ago.

Once upon a time you watched for me at the river's edge and I coming down from the mountains forgot you were there.

Each stone I selected by the water's edge held perhaps the mark of a rune the missing pieces of storyland told to you not what but how I could find you watching the fitting together of granite and miscellaneous scree how they fit together no-one was supposed to see.

Finally with a sigh I held my long purple skirt sideways across my knees stories and one simple message trapped in its folds and crept nearing to the campsite and started a fire. You were there by this time I was aware a spirit reaching up from the darkness to grasp my hand pull yourself upwards but I forgot again to listen to your wailing I had an infant to nurse and I must forever disregard your curse.

You who inhabit this knob and kettle topography
breathe not of your fiery demons, an exercise
in deflecting me from seeing at all: I should
have seen it coming, she told us long ago.

Winter Morning Sunrise

shadows from the winter stars
fall east and west

tears wet my cheeks
haloes of burning bushes
light the way

the way is of a morning such as this
secret special perfect fun
sight of the barbed wire crossing
sound of the dogs passing through
old path so familiar
shadows fall east and west

Father, You have made me

a daughter and a friend
but lately, you have made me my husband's wife,
and like to call me mom

I am the new mom
in her absence, I must peel potatoes,
wash carrots, fold laundry, vacuum

the cluttersound of homemaking
a comfort so real you'd rather stay in our cramped den
than return to the silence of your own home

Father, you have made me, and when Dad and I go to church
we sit together in our grief and cry

if this is not forever, this life, Dad asks
what did you and Mom talk about at night?
I would go to bed and you two sat upstairs for hours
trying to capture some essence of her now that she's gone

what did we talk about? oddly, of life and death
conversations foreboding and ominous in retrospect
yet comfortingly open-ended, the talking goes on

Dad, I can pretend that Mom is still upstairs waiting for me
comforting, real, ready with the next deep question

circling her knee with her index finger
twirling the tingles on her skin, this life, this body
it is for ever and ever a mystery. Dad, let's pretend
that Mom's upstairs, perhaps in the sky
waiting for us with some of the answers

Paintings

If I could frame in the words, make
something lasting, visible, enjoyable
something worthwhile for you to remember
would you want to see it?

a farmhouse painted in the family's absence
five white birches in the foreground
"each tree for one of us," Mom told me

out the den window watch
Dad shovel the circular driveway

deer trot up and around a faraway knoll
revealing
a herd of more than five

when he comes in we go downstairs
to pack up more of the backroom
"what about these canvasses
and this old portfolio?" I ask

Tied between two old boards
are sketches, oils, studies and paintings
mother has never shown us

Dogs and Horses

Granny sniffs when she's indignant
dogs and horses, she says,
there were always dogs and horses around

Dad called a collie Pal,
and when I ran down 9th street,
he'd hold my hand in his mouth
walk with him. Wait outside the Princess Theatre endlessly

the boys, Aly, and Jim, flitting out of the darkness
alley, back door, home.
Pally waiting at the front door of the theatre

Granddad knew horses, gave Aly a leg up. Aly
trains Jim's horses now and the big stallion
run on big bay, you are once and for always
in your wake there will be other dogs and horses
for the boys, their elders before them run on

alley, back door, home

Letter From Home

"Janet, I love you
will you come to Canada
and we'll get married?"

Why would I do such a thing?
You wonder, don't you?
Whether it's all planned out for you.

What is planned out for you, Granny?

Everything. Your life. You wonder
whether God has it all planned out for you

George wrote and asked me to come to Canada
He was not favoured by my mother

Those Thomsons. Always
had dogs and horses around

So my mother wanted me to marry another,
the manager of the furniture store
in Cambuslang
He was very respectable

who knows why we do the things we do
maybe it's all planned out for us anyway

Geordie Thomson wrote to Jenny Scott
Granddad to Granny

so here I am
part of the grand, divine plan

Boxing Day

On Boxing Day
we bundled up
dashed down the steps
to the warming car
sped away from the Christmas house
sped down Loch End Road

the pavement in icy hills
opening up before us

turned east to the city
at the 1A
and joined the queue
of nameless travelers
in new Camrys and pick-ups
racing into town

At Charleswood Drive
we left the Crowchild
merged with residential traffic
slowed past Banff Trail School
with the snowflakes taped to classroom windows
joined Auntie Norma and Uncle Russell
for holiday talk family news
and Christmas baking

news from the country: cold and snow
from the family: snow in London, England

midnight phone calls getting through
early evening reminiscences
as the real snow gathered out the picture window
behind the Xmas tree
and Auntie Norma showed us new paintings
evocative atmospheres of ducks in the mist
holiday talk
family news
(John got a raise
Jeff's started college)
and Christmas baking
("I made the white cake
but bought the dark")
a single day
in a single year
packed down like winter snowfall
icy hill of memory
slide down on cardboard boxes

Corrals

The wind across the corrals
may speak a lonely word or two

There's no one left to listen
The horses stayed down in the wooded fields
and did not come home last night

The snow in the corrals
and across the road

has covered every hoof print

the wind along the fencelines
under the graveled eaves
a silent kind of moaning
circling us in

Wind Chimes

ask me for a few words about the confluence
and I shall have to answer with two:
moon and sun. However, be it not said that the silence
of the stars the chimes of the wind along the pipes, the blue
night fading into day would have to be mentioned too

you only asked for two, didn't you?

auburn, russet, and gold, like the flight from that city of old
I've had my reasons for holding my tongue, you
can't imagine the wrath I've withheld simply by letting go
out into the field where a confluence, not just of stars
but of mars and Aries and thousands of nameless templars
have fought, loved, died in the glory of conflicting power
energy released beyond the stars, the night grows cold
under my hand the pages turn down script after script
and the powers grow old, though not nearly as old as their origins
and I've already told more than I know

think only of this: one kiss
bow down
arms akimbo, slight breeze in the air, the air bitingly cold
and hot, hold that thought for as long as a breath
and speak not a word of this till your death

Wisdom of Youth

a point of gold on the nethermost branch
I shift
crack of dry wood underfoot
in the muted forest

it is gone, sun behind a cloud

replaced by years of debris
floated down
eroded, packed, transmuted
replaced with the alchemy of age
leaden with this golden light
this burden

and in that loneliness one finds in the midst of one's peers
I find truth in my friends
only after and before
my tribal gatherings
my mind swept by guffaws and frivolities
basketball games
high school
big dreams

walking down by the creek at night to the camp
stomping around a campfire
everyone talking telling a story
interjections of humour
Gladstone and Bardwell
Gary Urban isn't even with us any more
some angel
the girls thought so
I could always spot his red Woods coat
who was it fell in the fire? Anyway
Gary may have had the utmost in wisdom
his youth,
angelic suicide
and walking away from the campfire
there are points of light in the sky

Carson and I are creeping up, behind cut branches
sneakers, laughing and serious
what a game we played

the creek

something like not really knowing the way to the camp
but setting off anyway
and falling through the huge forest
hearing the creek
moving toward several crossings
everything opening up

remember the aching cold treading
through the rivulets, crossing in deep places
bare feet
pants rolled up above the knees
five or six girls in the intense dry heat
wending through and over the water
waterways wending
the creek
the camp
the wisdom of youth

The Evolution of the Sand Tides

Out along the breakers
the dog fishes, the child peers through the water
the father stands with hips thrust forward
his hands there, his eyes wide

head thrown back at the glory of the blue day

where the broom holds sand cliffs high
I edge around boulders and sand
cling to the solidity of Earth, refute the sea

and my sister flits past, runs on
down the beach

can I ever catch up with her?

where the waves roll back there is a patch of sand

I take it
and run

family finally together
we find there is more to this ocean
than meets the eye
where the waves roll back there is another patch of sand
that grows as the tide goes out
children and parents come down with their pails
marvel at a seashell
shriek at spider crabs

we were once and always children there

Goddess

still and all there is the goddess
is she at the sea inside of me?

or at some stiller clearer calmer pool
not even a tidal pool, just water in a basin

almost amber in colour as it catches daylight
dawn on me, mother

with your own curative powers
sunlight at night

walk through the gate to the garden
and in that peaceful sanctuary

overwrought by overhead electrical lines,
say a prayer

tend the ash and the fire
I am so tired of sewing

at night my husband wakes
moaning about someone chasing after him

his sword
my tapestry, weaving this spell

set upon us, thank god, the hand that holds the sword
unraveling out of the ocean

no
weaving

Termagant

dfn. *termagant—a shrew; a woman with a violent, scolding, or nagging temperament; a scold. probably identified with* scrautum, *leather quiver for arrows*

The termagant my horoscope warned of
was me, I was the one with the spearing tongue
directing my aim, hunting it down

and tossing my head with casual ease
expecting to be reasonable and understood
it worked
I subdued the irrational
brought reason to the killing grounds

and I'd had no wish to hunt
trophies did not excite me, the smell
of blood luring the snowy owl
repelled me
and Enalyion and I trotted down the lane way
dawn breaking red across the murderous sky
we passed the hunter's yard

blood on the snowbank, entrails reeking
in the garbage pail
Enalyion had that startled, alarmed look
I was afraid that as a coy-dog she'd go wild on me

an owl swooped off the rafters of a garden shed
skimmed by and flapped
off behind neighbouring fir and spruce

later that day driving by the river
I saw again a five point stag
noble and aloof in the white and brown field

a flock of two or three hundred snow geese
bypassed that field flying low, overhead

I felt hunted, as if I was meant to see
the lingering fall of the shooting star
Orion? I wondered, could I have witnessed a spectacular fall?
No, not for me, the quiet calm acquiescence
I was made to be a kind of hunter
hunting simple words, enjoying the feasting dance
celebrations, untimid altercations

Orion above the barn
left spaces in which to dance, but
not yet for me, those stars

I turn my back on the barn
every night, drive away
back into the city

Yet I am always open for rejoinder, for
idle aloofness along the river bank
now that I've fought my way away

Moss, and Holiness Too

a spirit of this place
in large lake
lodge pole pine
uninhabited realm of mind
of mountains
staggering scree
fungus growing and old moss
ripping away from the rock face

a place so simple with subtle syllables
whispering
across the tops of the pines
by the wave-lapped shore
and rocks of mind
mystified by the whole process going on
and being a part of it, absorbed
slowly by the forces of decay and beauty

chanting out or silently
a raised hand to signal hello
a recognition and acceptance
in a brief notion
of understanding, pale
as the sunlight through trees
or at night, thin as ice heard

above
the rustling sound of feet through leaves

on the lake as a momentary dwelling place:
in the mind
those high places
where raptors soar over the pine-brushed floor
of the swift-cloudy sky

drinking at the height of the lake
having traced its gentle curves
ascending to the contours of the mind find

where a voice,
still reservoir voice
is

The Dancer

Artifice, a flung word on a heap of bones
burned away the truth in a fire.
The ring of stones stupefied the cattle
who shit indiscriminately while the hawk
circled above my world and a dancer
came to pas de deux among the crocus.

Hillside upon lavender hillside blooming crocus
petals push through snow and bones
the snow white and the flower soft like the foot of the dancer.
Bits of skin were singed in the fire.
South of the stones and higher, the hawk
circled away from the coming of the cattle.

Sometimes in the fog a man calls to the cattle
Ho-ome come ho-ome and they turn upon the crocus
trample everything, even the fallen nest of the hawk.
They ignore where coyotes have dug the bull-calf bones.
In the quiet that remains I feed the fire
wrap my cloak about my shoulders and look for the dancer.

Down in the valley there are five coyotes who circle the dancer
I hold my growling dog to me but she too smells of cattle
when out of the fog comes a man with eyes of fire
in his hand he holds a crocus.
I ward off his lovely spell with an amulet, bones
can be more trusting than the feather of a hawk.

The image shrieks and turns into a hawk
and all the while the coyotes circled the dancer
I would look tomorrow for his bones
out there trod upon by cattle.
He could not forever dance between the crocus
and I could not wait here with a heart full of fire.

I have lived beside the fire
tended the ring of stones beneath the hawk
watched my mother sketch among the crocus
waited eternally to be petitioned by the dancer
who died no better than a bull calf among cattle.
And I have found no trace of bones.

His fire was all artifice, his bones
his hawk-like face, all trod upon by cattle.
The simple crocus too plentiful for the dancer.

Shards

I knelt in a landscape lit by overworld colours
one knee up, one bent almost to the ground
my bluejeans tucked into pale suede boots
my hair curled around my tanned face
my long sleeved arm clad in an embroidered shirt
reaching
down for a shard of the mirror of sleep
that mirror that broke again last night

to face in that shard an old memory
she was Katie in the seventies,
a woman who basked lizard-like on a rock by the river
in the Idaho sun, she had hair that curled about her face too
and she wore a long burgundy skirt, an Indian cotton blouse
high suede boots

and Katie took up with me - I had the white Volkswagen
the Bruce Cockburn tapes from Canada
the will to travel up rutted isolated mountain paths
to her sunshine friends doing yoga on the grassy downs
to her sister's place in Moscow
university town and the sauna scene sisters of the moon
          sweating, sharing and story-eyed
to the fairgrounds
   to the starry night in the farmland—where, I don't know where

and the piece of memory shining in my hand
flickering on my face, eyes open or closed
revealed so little about myself
I wondered what stroke of fate
broke that mirror hanging over me
moved my hand to select that particular splinter of the past

the broken, forgotten, ill-pieced past
there but for the memory of it
go I

In the Sky

up against the rock face
where the ochre sun slips into shadow
a shining aircraft zooms
leaving behind a white trail
black see-through shadows
etch themselves against the face

your craggy smile
inarticulate gesturing
show fear
of a tin god with white plumes
zooming against the blue

I thought of Carlos Casteneda this morning
when the crow flew down the laneway between rows of trees

backyards fenced in by mythologies of suburban bliss
I thought also of Tolkein's black and feeding birds

I thought simply of the neighbourhood, the cool fall morning
and how the occasional something in flight is always a relief

from the rain strewn ground
a reason to look up

upon primitive articulations of the gesturing

Innocence

Something about being imagistic and concrete
about providing you with the dramatic moment
terrifies me because there is so much to say
so little to leave out, but I'll try.

It's like trying to spot the little lights flashing around in the garden
the glinting sunlight and "The Hissing of Summer Lawns"
Joni Mitchel soundtrack playing on the patio
while I sit and watch the coming storm

there are wisps of clouds hanging onto the mountains
Yamnuska looks particularly inviting through the binoculars
I watch the wisps move from peak to peak and think of being
on the other side
in Nelson where you're actually in the wisps as they move

and the prairie grasses undulate in the warmth of the wind
I use an Indian tomahawk head to hold my papers down
on the patio, the sun over my shoulder
writing about essentials and watching the ducks
the cows   the grasses

growing tall like the mountains
shifting a little as the earth moves
and feeling very godlike
in this sane effort to testify to my innocence

finding the soul inside me to be the constant I found as a child
being a child with my sister in the fields, the Engliosh Club
membership including cats and dogs with capes
little girl passwords, dance steps in the wind

later, coming home from university,
walking down into the field
throwing my toque up into the coming wind
catching it boomeranging back

later, still, walking with my husband-to-be
traversing the barb-wire
going down into the forest, silent and watchful
holding hands and silent

since then, the lines have changed
bardic and epic, those goodbyes on the driveway,
an old friend unbelieving as the words spew from my mouth
my lifeline, I told him, indicates a violent death

protestations of innocence notwithstanding
the dreams of my memory continue
enduring slings and arrows
misfortune and aging as everything continues, this drama on earth

Erosion

Long grasses rustle in the field today
I try to sway too
seated on the moving earth
a hillside underneath the hawks.

Somehow in the back and forth
disquiet disrupts
and I turn upon myself.
The wind's language is no newer to me
than the symbols in this poem
not intentionally symbolic but inherently so.

Perhaps as I rehearse my thoughts they shall
erode a little
being less and less
of the same thing
to go over
in

Lineage

Gods

Where are you running?
From whence have you come?
okay yodel raven call
come tell me some news
of timepieces and tapestries
and fine sleet through the mist

Psalmistry

We do not know when the world will end
few of us have studied the prophecies
those who have say soon

soon the end of economic bondage
soon the age when talents are recognized.

Who wrote the song, creates the chants.
We all repeat and begin to believe, we ask
who wrote that song?

Does it matter that the devil
is his own muse?

And the women write to free themselves
begin to believe.
The men stop their ears
to matriarchal language. The evolving
species
stops.

No,
one cannot manipulate destiny
manuscript of lifelines on hands.

What mantlepiece in heaven
could compare to our hearthpiece
stacks of manuscripts
fed to flames.
Burn the technical reports, and chaos
is still a brute fact.
Snakes begin to speak with men
that knowledge is chaos.

The god inside men wrings her hands
there can be no flowering
if no-one tends the garden.
Her hands caught up in the weaving,
a god makes garments for war kings
nurses the knowledge of her pregnancy
and the men of destiny
create guidance controlled
missiles.

The shepherd has lost his sheep, there is no wool left
there is no wool left to weave.

The mind of men encompasses
the universe
and when the nova bursts
war starts
and in the flames the lies die down
ashes sift.

A rattler moves
onto the sun warmed hearth stones.

New Sightings in Sight

Only when I look at them are they gone.
Only from the corners of my eyes are they visible
for any length of time

Simple glances of them prolong or vanish unexpectedly
throughout the calmness of the day

Oh yes I have seen the quick and vanishing
species of spirits: foothills. full-moon, wind-blown
careful creatures.

Covering quite a range of themselves, they have
descended the spectrum arching from my fingertips
to where kestrels cry this side of the mountains.

It's their visible proximity that's important.

Whew! Once they stand still, I can focus:
then they're glimpsed over willow tops, gone into oblivion.

When as if that bald eagle in the Kootenays knew
the exact location of the gateless gate, he grew
great in the cottonwood for a moment then grasped
a shaft of sunshine, evaded the showers and ascended
the spiral which spread across the lake.

That was mountain time and one of the first moments
my vision pierced the gates.

Profuse loon laughter here in the foothills
with the spirits assembled according to geomantic forms. Earthy

That is to say, it's the spectrum they are on: the
physics of birdsong, the extent of desire,
the angle of a shadow.

Where do these things come from, where do they go?

Laughter, possibly to distract, fails because of new wisdom
founded on looking for nothing.

Yes somehow still within my peripheral vision (even
here in a re-cognized sighting of them seeming to fly
over the barley, crawl through high timothy, or walk among aspen.)

The sound of their movement is silence, and an aha
as my body continues arching and breathing, arching and breathing,
unsupposing, as I expect them but do not watch for them.

Ah! the barn-yard fixtures, the fence posts unpainted
and porcupines hiding there, the pigeons and the poop.
Red painted plywood boxstalls, polyethylene covering the hay,
black rubber tubs and goldfish filled water troughs.

All of these things extemporaneous
until one of those odd creatures comes,
a firefly darkening the day.

Finding Boundaries

I have felt cabin bound
and bushed
shivered the night away
talking philosophy

I have searched the fencelines
for trespassers

searched the flightpath of gyrfalcons in winter
for habits, routines of hunt and seek
caught a wink of red
beneath the fencepost roost
in the skiff of snow there are feathers and red ice

crossed the fencelines
with philosophy striding at my side
once a year I search
for evidence
for barbed wire loopholes
a way out

enchanting talk of European travels
fails to warm me
am I impoverished, sedentary
here by the rundlestone hearth, fire blazing?
This anniversary leaves for another year,
I walk the fields
watch jets pass overhead
watch for aurora borealis
watch the sun rise
and the sun set
this binds me to myself
and all that lives within the borders
of this twenty acres

In the End

Now I can't get back to that space
rocking, rocking
reading all that stuff about Hermes the thrice born

I can't get inside that magic
perhaps it's inside of me
dreamy and veiled

like a bride with her whole life ahead of her,
dreamy and veiled, unless
carousel rocking horse, red and black
the why in this night of wings and effigies
answered by a truth

stay at home
cultivate your garden
long ago and far away you answered

I forgot

In the end, there is a beginning
simple truth, that
magic? what not
not true, just simple
magic and truth
the here and now, never ending
amen

giddy-up Andrew, giddy-up

Life Sentence

We gave them life
in a prison of ancient words
those criminal gods of old
improvised a poetry
to reveal their passionate deeds

their crimes were to love with no reason
love Love
the only god with no parents

and the ancient kings and queens
disturbed in their tombs by our very musings
transmigrated, perhaps
through an alchemy no one recalls
(take this, and eat)

recall how tiny statues of gods and goddesses
graced every hearthplace
and waken to toss off their breastplates
bronze and silver bracelets
a token for the river gods

plunder is perpetual, eternal
and surely the gods have need
of none of these baubles or hopes
(human frailties and lusting after things)

after all, is what makes us human
this placelessness we call love?
or is it who you love and why?

even the wantonness of indeterminacy
leaves you asking for more
we can never have enough and yet
how often have I said that sometimes
even love is not enough?

transcend this kinship we feel for one another then
and yield, be pliant within the family of gods

of ancient tombs
there is little of substance left anyway
every talisman sacrificed in the passing crime called love

even the Pyramid itself, treasure trove of the divine architect
with its mathematics wielded into stone
worthless and priceless all at once
immaterial, blessed and holy

what receptacle in my possession is holy enough
for Calendula, Artemisia, Absinthium?

I need an altar
a kneeling ground for falling down

oh Love,
pour forth thy goodness
here and here
into this cradle of deep wound
the wound where birthing and loneliness
reveals a lovely land
so lonely and terrible

only my ancestors in their multitude
and you and me, searching
for the fallen gods can find

a tomb that isn't a tomb
the monument to mother's death
that copse of aspen and willow
ashes scattered and roses blooming

(plunder the past for a story, and read on)
this sentence that isn't a sentence
but life itself, in holy words

Poetry of the Ancients

Boccaccio at the ocean
watches the sacred whale dance
in the confluence of a full moon, Big Dipper
moon irradiating what remains of a rainbow moonbeam
whales surfacing and breaching in a circle
phosphorescent light offshore

Boccaccio on the continent
a trio of wolves down from the mountains
moves through on its way to Montana
tracked by little radar beams in round collars
pausing after a kill to circle each other in song

Boccaccio, you believed in a race of men descended from the gods
ancient poetry, after all, was synonymous with theology
divinely inspired, bardic, epic, valiantly moral
the gods lived the myths and copulated with mere mortals
their stories, myths, realities veiled by the metres of rhyme
alas, the myths are alive, only on paper
wafer thin sacraments of words

dust blowing across abandoned tipi rings
story-skins
petroglyphs, a genealogy of gods

Chinooks, rainbows
arches, encompassing, not circling
wheeling hawks

Boccaccio in Canada
with no-one to tell about it
defend poets and poetry
help us form a circle to sing praises

Husband, Stag and Free

Husband Honorifics

After all of the yearning, you came to stand at my office door
the steps up over the sill trippable, bound to change you

finally entered the little book-lined room, poked around my purse
found *The Imagist Poet* tucked between folds of leather

opened the book to DH Lawrence and read aloud
your voice so rich and sure, enunciating

if I wasn't yet sure you were the one
I knew later when you lifted my foot

knee bent backward your hand on my knee
checking the heel of my black pump

nothing too sexual, just practical
as a blacksmith might check a shoe

At What Hour Does Morning Come?

When the morning comes
sunlight illuminates the mountains
electrifies the fields

bulls wary of fences

black and white woodpecker
with hatch of red
feeds at balcony suet

and porcupine clings to willow tree

the windows
visibly frosted
make raindrops over the view
someone showers
the coffee burbles and perks

at what hour do I say that I love thee?
at what hour does the morning begin
was it "last night" at three
with the icy moon on the blue floral carpet
or at seven
when the sun shone
slowly across the marble floor

Arrow

sounding

out
tuning fork
vibration
hand flutters in extension
over to you
my quiver
ing continues   through each heartbeat
is controlling like rhythm control

the line between you and me
the expanse no extended hand can close
fire me
expand

target-seeker

Constellation

the arrow, once dislodged to fly again
will find you
you are its target and I, I am the archer
a blind tool in the hand of fate
a bow, akimbo with slender flexibility bending
wending my arms to flail out in a falling reflex, stop me
stop it

in flight, the sound is a ringing in my ears
I play soft Narada music
enter the script of my own movie the music is evocative
makes tears whip out of the corners of my eyes
my eyeglasses are spattered with warm tears my ears
are full of this sound this ringing in my ears

call me
telephone
answering machine catches the memos
the echoes of another time

is it possible to live like this
always in flight
always seeking out the target
the bulls eye even I can't see
my head down I am in flight, rushing toward
the constellation of my family
clustered in the night

I Watch You Sleeping

You did not wake
when the great wedge went over
nor did your slumber cease
as the storybook morning, chapter after chapter,
revealed its magic.

You did not wake
though the mountains stood crystalline
as the sun illuminated the distant range
and flock after flock sounded their trumpet cries
over the rolling prairie hills

Stag

as I said, I let my hair down
allowed the wild threat of luck loose
like driving on an icy road
and seeing shining eyes ahead
I can't stop on the narrow bridge
the coulee's below, the ice is ahead
the snow is blowing
I am alone in the perfect night

he walks slowly across the road
then stands squarely to watch me speed past
a fine five point stag

I stay my course
letting only the wild night be
you have found me
you on the other side of the light
observe your own wild maiden
in her garden
my husband, stag
and free

words are no longer important
we do not watch what we do
the night, the garden, life is speeding past
outside, the clipped ice of our rapid passing
whirls around the starlight
touching all the loose creatures of the night

Stairway

You know, I don't remember a thing that you said

I'm sorry, I don't recall anything you said yesterday
on the telephone
I was having a deja vu. You'd think
that having heard it twice I would have at least
remembered it
but twice blessed with having
heard the story, I can only remember the ending
something about a stairway
and a chandelier

I'm telling you about a stairway
and there are wolves howling outside
the highland bagpipes on my tape recorder
are frenzied but oddly, Celtically controlled
I couldn't explain the music and the mood and the steps I've taken
again
even if I wanted to—which I do—I can't see the way
it's sad, but
the steps are fading, the stairway has completely
wound up into itself

deja vu did it with such clarity
that the air was a clarified white
could have been the snow and it was
the solitude of being behind glass

walls of snow coming down outside
reflections of the light drifting
into my office the miracle of telephone
contact connect
your voice
those things you said
the stairway
circular and empty
outside under the chandelier
of sky
I denied ever having seen a wisp
of blue of you navy, teal, Merlin
azure and how little it mattered
after all, your suit colour
your navy-blue shape on the fading steps
an evening of mystery sweeping down the stairs
out of the sky, like Orion over the windowsill
marching down with his dog
night after night

tell me that story again

Step By Step

We pass on the stairway
you and I
pausing to take hand in hand
a pass
lateral movement to allow others by
a brief exchanged hello
tingle left in the air
dog on the stair
breaks us apart
good day
it is fair to say
this did not happen yesterday
you pulled your long coat in closer
to hug yourself
hand on the banister
eyes up and ahead to the landing

warning
not all is as it seems below

So be careful on those steps!
My father warns again and again
in spite of all these warnings
I fall five or six steps
the baby cradled in my arms
my husband rushes to see what has happened
thump thump thumpy bump
identifiable sound, somehow
even this noise is not enough
I imagine mother still sitting there
in the orange floral chair
and we think we can hear her bang on the wall for help
we can see her sitting on the steps
above the makeshift crib
a little girl in white

So don't fall down the steps
be careful of the ghost on the steps
the spirit from another world
be true to yourself and sure on your feet
cradle the baby in your arms
and turn no deaf ear to any charms

Symbolic Poetry

I let it come
and like an idea
it grows on paper, the complexities
enrich, entwined, confound

I let it come and the empty pages fill
the sense of accomplishment
my own true love
I let it come for you

and all I want to write
the philosophical
the mute individual defenses
the factual, the biblical
the historical and new
fade into prose
and all I see is a metaphor of you

Merlin

we saw the Merlin
she was high and overhead
off to the north
flying east, darting west
her latitude defined by the river valley

the trees and the fluid slopes the river wrought
a mapped message for her flight
readable signs, undeniable guides

we saw the Merlin, she was aloft
and we were walking under a canopy
of tall, majestic bare elms
fir trees
the mountain ash still held their berries above the snow

we walked, plotted our course through the forest
alone, we walked, you and I
and as we walked, our tuning fork thoughts
charming the trees
beside the fluid slopes of the river
a quick grey shadow darting overhead

Motherhood

My birth is not by any act of theirs, those principles of higher ancestry, but as they contemplate themselves I come to birth.

What, then, does this mean? That what we call Nature is Soul, child of a prior Soul more potently alive, a Soul at peace and in possession of an inner vision, with neither upward nor yet downward tendency, but reposing in its being, its own stillness and awareness of itself, and in this consciousness and self-awareness it beholds its own progeny, to the limit of its powers, and has no further aim than the noble and delightful spectacle it has perfected.

Enneads, by Plotinus, *III 8.iv*

The Mythology of Landscape

How can I say there is a mythology of the landscape?
If there is can we say it begins at birth?
Surely not, for such a belief denies motherhood
        mother earth
        mother nature
the creation of each new life
Yet it is the grown child who creates mythologies, isn't it?

This morning I lay in the warmth of my husband's arms
I felt the baby move in the orbit of its landscape
I may never again be this connected
to another life
unless the paper this is penned on
outlives my life
unless there is
a mythology of the landscape
that I may return to
my baby a grown child walking the earth
with mythologies of uncertain origin haloing the ground
my flesh and bones turned to the dust of earth

if so, I would that I may, flesh and bones and dust
create within the womb of my earth
a landscape for the living
a mythology that endures
a prayer for the living

Swimming

Still sitting
the emotion of everwhelming motherhood
washes over the water
emanating from within
wave after wave
pulls me deeper into the pool
I am moved by the buoyancy

the baby swims within
small splashes of sound

in the deep pool my hair wet on my skull
the clear water

not long now

Baby Focus

The prenatal books prescribe imminent emotions
which I scoff at for their prescriptive nature
I shall feel as feelings
fall
naturally upon myself
I shall be natural
and complete
without
preconceived
notions or ideals

yet this focus
inward
is in a true sense
accurately described—inward to my baby
squirreling, swimming, hiccuping
kicking up under my ribs
eating everything
that I eat
an ingestion machine

I am focused in on you babe
on your nursery
your clothes
all that I can do to make you safe and warm
my deep breaths of fall air
bi-weekly swims
happy thoughts
regular, nutritious meals
long walks with Enalyion
conversation
music
quiet
all that I can do
focusing
in
on
you

Mornings

Some mornings the silence
velvet and stolen like the night is
still and soft around me
I waken to the rainfall falling outside
and the dark pavement glistens under the lamplight
the dog, let out, noses about in the underbrush
and comes in with black wet paws
her golden coat dripping and flecked with bits of leaves

I wear my pyjamas around the silent house
switch on the lights as I move from room to room
searching for the last vestiges of last night
there's nothing there
the blackness fades
the rainclouds lift
sun streams in through the window slats

Linearity

Even with an orderly arrangement of ideas
these thoughts skip through my head like arrows

materializing as shafts of feathered realities
ancient and troubling with insistent targets
determining perpetual motions, moods, behaviors

the labour of giving birth
the startling debilitating ache and pain afterwards
indeterminate ideas about gods and spirits floating
contracting and expelled like a breath or worse, like lochia

our world isn't so very plain after all
the orderly arrangement of things tampered with
realigns and corrects itself
as we plummet headlong toward a chaotic target
lusting after the proper order, the essence of things

Mother and Child

on the far-wall
my shadow
woman's head and shoulders

with baby's head at left shoulder
the night grows older

baby bobs to sleep
carried on rhythmic footfall

morning light diffuses shadows in the roomlight

through the door pane watch
blue moonlight through pine trees
winter ice crystal haloes
gone up in the air
like blue night light

and the blanket of snow outside
pure angel white
holding not even the shadow of a footprint

Stairway

dna soul
of a higher rank

climber

trellis, vine, riverbank

wine in a goblet, this kinship
diviner

yield, being pliant
the writ

speak of land, future tenses
death and taxes

illumination, our world is a beacon
ramification?

dna, limit perfectly
cancer

soul, of a higher rank
flight

and indeterminacy, whither?
whiter

up and down the spiral
entwined

proper position of the soul
trajectory

encompass this self
soul

goal? transcendent, extrinsic
intrinsic

dna soul
all one's own

Spring Rain

the mauve of green
fields where the heifers last summer
ate to the first layer of top soil
earth on their muzzles
where now buffalo beans bloom
the clumps of wet grass green
miraculously rained upon rolling slopes
the enclave of a pond by orange willow
and muskrats even plopping in the rain
their coats as furrowed as the fallow fields:
not but roughened and likened to fields

spring in all the obvious places
dark currents of weeds and brine shrimp
frogs in the muck
and the smell of sweet grass on a horse's mouth
honey bees fertilizing with their legs

walking in the rain over anthills
gopher holes and the purple reminder
of a divinity lost in the stars
flooded out through the trap-door of earth
dispersed in this precipitation
not forgotten in this closing of eyes.

Printed in February 1997 by
VEILLEUX
ON DEMAND PRINTING INC.
in Boucherville, Quebec